My
EVER-PRESENT LORD

My
EVER-PRESENT LORD

Penelope J. Thiel

*True Accounts of
God's Love, Sense of Humor,
and Miraculous Intervention*

TATE PUBLISHING *& Enterprises*

My Ever-Present Lord
Copyright © 2011 by Penelope J. Thiel. All rights reserved.

No part of this publication may be reproduced, stored in a retrieval system or transmitted in any way by any means, electronic, mechanical, photocopy, recording or otherwise without the prior permission of the author except as provided by USA copyright law.

Scripture quotations are taken from the *Holy Bible, King James Version*, Cambridge, 1769. Used by permission. All rights reserved.

The opinions expressed by the author are not necessarily those of Tate Publishing, LLC.

Published by Tate Publishing & Enterprises, LLC
127 E. Trade Center Terrace | Mustang, Oklahoma 73064 USA
1.888.361.9473 | www.tatepublishing.com

Tate Publishing is committed to excellence in the publishing industry. The company reflects the philosophy established by the founders, based on Psalm 68:11,
"The Lord gave the word and great was the company of those who published it."

Book design copyright © 2011 by Tate Publishing, LLC. All rights reserved.
Cover design by Lauran Levy
Interior design by Sarah Kirchen
Photography by Dr. William Birkby

Published in the United States of America

ISBN: 978-1-61739-950-3
1. Religion / Christian Life / Inspirational
2. Biography & Autobiography / Religious
11.04.06

With great honor and thanks, this is very gratefully dedicated to Jesus Christ, my LORD, Savior, and Best Friend, without whom this book very obviously would not have been possible.

Table of Contents

Preface 9
Free at Last! 11
God Knows Where You Live 19
So, What Are Firstfruits? 25
Little Blacky 37
It's the Little Things 53
You Can't Do That! 'Cause
You're a Girl! That's Why! 57
Life around the Lake 69
Last Week I Went to Hell 77
Aaaaah Yes... the Cigarettes 85
And Then...God Gave Me a Sign 103
You Can Lead a Heart to Water 109

Preface

So...this little book has found its way into *your* hands. You are *most blessed* indeed! This has been written especially for you. No matter who you are, where you come from, or what you believe. Yes, *you!*

Take a moment to feel the weight of it in your hands and maybe even feel of one of the pages between your thumb and forefinger. Relax. Let it become kind of a part of you ... a friend.

What you are about to read is all true. They are accounts taken from my daily journals I've been keeping since 1982. I am currently working in journal 117.

I don't call these "stories" because that, to me, implies there may be areas of partial truths, and this is certainly not the case with what is written here. You may start reading with your mind, but you will eventually come upon something that must be considered with your heart—where the spiritual forces of faith, hope and love reside. The strengths of God.

These are all simple accounts of how God has shown Himself to be so strong and very present in my life over the past years. Great is His love and faithfulness, but also great are His methods and sense of humor.

Please get to know Him and see Him in these pages. Listen for His voice in your heart. His word says that the things of God are for "whosoever will." You certainly qualify as a "whosoever," but the question is, "*Will* you?"

Sometimes catch the preachin' that was goin' on the Trinity Broadcasting channel.

One, two, sometimes three o'clock in the morning just praising God. Sometimes singin' at the top of my lungs. Proudly quotin' scripture to my cat. Havin' the time of my life and just *totally plastered*, but *surely* saved!

Every day and evening, it was the same scenario. Day after day ... after day. This went on for a year. Yeah, at *least* a year. Unbelievable.

Now then, I do not remember the date, but I can tell you this: I don't even remember comin' home. All I know is that "when I came to myself" (you'll find that in Acts 12:11, when Peter suddenly came to the realization that an angel had escorted him out of prison) I was sittin' in my den with everything as usual: Bible open, Bible cards close at hand ... but ... I didn't have my wine. Let that sink deep into your heart. I ... *did not* ... have my wine.

What a moment. I still get misty and flooded with what I can only apply words to as being soooo, *so* grateful. It's like the LORD was standing there with His arms outstretched to me saying, "Penny, I have this gift for you. Would you like it?"

The stillness. As far as I can recollect, I just sat there for hours. Not sayin' anything. Just…quiet. Feelin' so little. So humble. So comforted. So secure. So blessed. So loved. There is no one like Him.

It was also my moment of truth. I could have sat there all stunned and surprised thinkin,' "Wow, I don't have my wine! I need to go get my wine!" But no, I was being overcome with a peace and comfort like I had never felt before and knowing that those addictive shackles were just melting off of me. I was *free at last*! Glory to God!

That has been over twenty years ago. You need to know that from that moment of freedom, I never *once* have had a craving for a drink. I actually didn't have any withdrawal symptoms at all. None *at all*. I should have been well into the DTs before the sun came up, but no. I was delivered and completely healed! I am *the healed* of the LORD!

I have come to realize that all of the study, seeking, and searching with a sincere heart little by little was replacing the darkness and addiction that permeated me with light and life. Eventually there was so much light there, the alcohol and darkness *had* to leave! I know you've heard that "God will meet you right where you are." Well, I was imprisoned in a horrible, suffocating pit. He came down into that pit with me and pulled me out. Thank You, Jesus!

I've been journaling over the past twenty-six years and countless recorded wonderful works of God are in those pages, but they are for another time. This has been written for your comfort, and that you might have hope.

If you are in cruel servitude to alcohol or drugs, *seek the* LORD and deliverance *will come*. It may not be *exactly* in the way He delivered me, but He's so creative, He'll have something tailored just especially for you. It *is* His will. He loves you and wants only the best for you.

God Knows Where You Live

I've been walking with the LORD for a while now, and there's one thing that never ceases to amaze me: sometimes He'll do something that is so 'Him' and there's no way around it. It *was* Him! You have to just sit, continue reliving it, thinking about it, shaking your head, and smiling.

Two weeks ago, we received notice that our boss's mom had passed away. I'm sure our workplace is not any different from your workplace. We decided to get a card for him and take up a collection. Evidently his mom was greatly devoted to the Salvation Army, and instead of flowers, the family wanted whatever money that was collected to go there as a memorial.

It was a Monday afternoon, and my laboratory manager quietly appeared in my office. She had a sympathy card in her hand and softly said, "Would you do this for me?" indicating that she wanted me to take care of the card and collection. Of course I didn't mind, but I thought it odd at the time that she would ask me. Usually it would have been given to one of the administrative assistants to handle.

So, through the week, I got the card all filled with signatures and got the collection done.

At the end of the week, last Friday actually, it was time to get it all put together. I got the home address for the card and looked up the address of our local Salvation Army office.

I was sittin' there with the money that was donated and decided to save myself the trip to the bank or local market for a money order and would simply write a check to the Salvation Army for the amount and take the cash. I remember smilin' as I put the money into my wallet. I never carry any appreciable amount of cash. That was more money than I had on me in a long, long time. I usually carry just a couple of bucks and have no idea of exactly how much I have in my wallet.

Saturday rolled in and I'll tell you what, it was my day to just *do it all*! I go ninety to nothin' on Saturday and this last Saturday, I had part of an ongoing project planned. I was going to hang some molding, chair rail, and finish some baseboards in the foyer and dining room. Had everything I needed. I was *ready*!

I'm working flat out getting lots done and behold: *I'm fixin' to run out of finish nails!*

No, no. I *do not* run out of nails! Please! And ya know how you can be just a goin' along real good and something like this will totally wreck your whole deal, break your stride, and be just a major inconvenience?

At this point I also noticed that I was gonna need an extra piece of baseboard that I could only get at Lowe's. Didn't need it right away, but hey, if I was gonna drop what I was doin' for a couple of packages of nails, I might as well get the baseboard at the same time.

Yep, I could have gone to Walmart. Yep, could have gone to Home Depot. The whole baseboard thing really had me feeling very mentally irregular. I was gonna have to go to Lowe's.

$98.00 *later*, I'm walkin' out to my truck havin' an *audible* conversation with the LORD. "Why is it you go in with plans that you're gonna just get a few things and walk away fully qualified for debtor's prison! What is it about these home improvement centers?"

So, I'm havin' this real good blah-blah with the LORD and this gal passes by me. It looks like she's just headed into Lowe's but no, she turns around and I hear, "Excuse me, Miss, can you help me?"

Odd. I smiled and answered her like I actually knew her, "Well, sure."

She walked over and as I was securing the molding in the back of my truck, she started tellin' me how she had just lost her job and had no place for her and her children to stay. She said $43.00 would get them a room for a week and that her husband had finally gotten a job and would be paid next Friday. I was listenin' as I was tying the molding down. She probably thought I wasn't listening at all, but see, I had already told her that I'd help her. I was hearin' her just fine.

Got everything done and quietly went into my purse for my wallet. Opened my wallet and there were two twenties and three ones.

I pulled out the money and was smilin' as I handed it to her and said, "There ya go. Forty three dollars."

Wow, if you could have seen the look on her face! She was speechless but managed after a few moments to eek out, "Thank you!"

With very intense eye contact, I reached out, firmly held her hands, and softly said, "Be blessed, and do good!"

As she walked away from me, I kind of followed after her with my eyes, but the parking lot was full and I lost sight of her.

Sure did find myself prayin' for her as I drove home, and you know what? I was about half-way home when I realized the check I had written on Friday for the Salvation Army was for exactly $43.00! Got so excited I wrestled and hassled gettin' my check book out of my purse while I was driving to look at my check register and yep, it sure was!

Gee, and then suddenly the whole orchestration of it started rollin' through my mind, all the way back to when my boss came to me and asked if I would take care of the card and donation. And the whole ridiculous nail thing! I sure wasn't smiling then but I am now.

What a feeling of security it gives me when I think about all of it. The bottom line here is that 2 Corinthians 9:10 rings true in that God *does* minister seed to the sower. And the extra added attraction? *God knows where you live!* He will also go to extravagant means to get you to the right place at the right time. He is just truly *amazing*. It was Him!

So, What Are Firstfruits?

I have always been a tither. Seems tithing is just about the first thing I heard after I got saved and just figured that when the Word says, "Bring ye all the tithes..." (Malachi 3:10), then that's what you should do. I've never had any qualms about tithing, even when it looked like I was goin' down financially and leavin' no bubbles. To stop tithing was *never* an option.

I've heard so many people say, "Well, I can't afford to tithe." No...you can't afford *not* to! I'm serious! God has monumentally blessed me for just the obedience in tithing alone. He honors His Word.

I could go on and on about tithing and offerings, but the odd thing is I've been saved over twenty years, and it wasn't until, say, maybe four years ago the pastor of the church I was attending actually had a sermon on first fruits.

I seem to remember hearing first fruits mentioned but just that, mentioned. There was never any teaching on it, not that I can remember anyway.

So, here I am some twenty-eight years down the road and out of the blue the pastor was preachin' on first fruits. You'll notice I said 'preaching' and not 'teaching.' There's a difference. Actually, it was a kind of a succotash 'cause he had tithing and offerings all mixed in with it.

On and on for the better part of an hour and a half, and the truly bizarre thing was he never really said how to figure out what your first fruit offering should be or how it's calculated. What I gleaned from it was you just give on your increase, like you just increased your tithe. Hum…but I had always done that.

There was something there that was makin' me go a little sideways in my heart. I made a mental note to ask pastor about it but then just kind of forgot.

It was about a month ago. I was in my prayer time, and behold, (you know how your mind can sort of drift when you're prayin'?) suddenly I'm sittin' there thinkin' about first fruits!

"Odd," I thought, but then continued, "Sir, would you please get first fruit information to me if it's something I'm missin' out on or not doin' correctly?"

I'll tell you what, it was the following week (big smile). I tape my TV preachin' line-up every morning and watch in the evening when I come home from work.

Prepare to be blessed!

Here's one of my favorite preachers of all time, and the first words out of his mouth? "So let's talk about first fruits."

"Yeah!" I yelled in hearty agreement.

I sat there watchin' with this huge grin on my face just feelin' *so special*. I always get answers from the LORD, but as I'm sure you know, sometimes answers can take a while. There's pretty much always a space of time between the "amen" and the "there it is."

But hey, after you put the "amen" on a prayer and three or four days later you have an answer? I call that *stylin'*!

So, what I'll do here is condense a thirty minute teaching into a few paragraphs. This is good now. :)

Here's our scriptures:

> And now behold, I have brought the first fruits of the land which You, O LORD, have given me. And you shall set it before the LORD your God and worship before the LORD your God.
>
> Deuteronomy 26:10

> And the first fruits of your land you shall bring into the house of the LORD your God.
>
> Exodus 23:19

> Honor the LORD with your substance and with the first fruits of all your increase; so shall your barns be filled with plenty and your presses shall burst out with new wine.
>
> Proverbs 3: 9–10

Now if you're feelin' a bit apprehensive because they are all Old Testament scriptures, I will direct you to Malachi 3, the most hugest tithing chapter of all time, and verse six: *"I am the* LORD *and I change not."* There, that ought to settle it.

So according to the teaching I heard, the first fruits is the first part of your increase. Let's say you get a dollar an hour raise. We're gonna put this on an eighty-hour pay schedule because pay is most commonly an every-two-week event. So, your increase will be $160 a month.

The first $160 extra is your first fruits, and that's what you give. Course you don't give it every month 'cause then it wouldn't be a raise at all. No, just the increase from the first two forty-hour paychecks that have your raise on them.

Clear so far, yeah? Easy, yes?

You know what I suddenly realized? When I bought a new home and rented out my old one a few years back, that first rent check was a rather large first fruits increase. I sat there knowing I owed God that first month's rent. Oh, I have been tithing on the increase, but after hearing an accurate, easily understandable explanation of first fruits, I realized

I sure did owe God that first month's rent. Ah...I also got a $1.33/hour raise that I had never paid on either.

Are you gettin' a grasp on what's goin' on here? This was parlayin' into more than just a little chump change. Did it make me a little uncomfortable? *Oh yeah!* 2 Corinthians 9:8 very clearly says that "God is able to make all grace abound toward you, that you *always*, having *all sufficiency* in *all things* may abound to every good work." That is very terrific, but the catch is in the verse before it: *"God loves a cheerful giver"* (9:7).

Just the simple act of giving should bless you. I have come to literally see a bird being liberated from my hand when I give. I heard a famous preacher say this, "You just open your hand and turn loose of that check and watch it fly away to multiply your harvest in your future." He also says, "When you open your hand, God opens His." I like that.

So yeah, I was gonna have to deal with my own heart and be sure that I was comfortable, giving cheerfully, and in faith, before I ever wrote that check.

Besides, when you have a strong inner witness about what God wants you to do and you *don't* do it? Hum...here I had asked him for some information, and zippity-do, there it was! For me to ignore it and get off into some carnal stupidity like, "Gee, I wonder if that really was God?" or "Gaaawd? If this is really you, please have a camel out in my front yard on Monday at 8:00 a.m." That would have been nothin' but stiff-necked disobedience!

God is not trying to take something from you! He's trying to get something to you!

I have watched Luke 6:38 ("Give and it shall be given unto you...") come to pass right before my very eyes so many times, and no, I'm not talkin' outrageous things like money fallin' out of the sky...which...actually, I guess is very closely akin to tax money in a fish's mouth, so hey, why limit God, huh?

Now I'm fixin' to share something with you that is just extraordinarily fun and was the LORD's direct response to my giving first fruits.

I gave my first fruits last Sunday, August 23, 2009. I was scheduled to go out to California the following Friday to see my aged, rapidly failing, most treasured Aunt Mary. I was staying with my cousin, Claudia.

I worked for Claudia during the years of 1998 to 2001 and also worked for a second employer during that time, which is the only time I have ever had a 401K.

So, I'm visiting with my cousin in her kitchen that following Friday evening, and she goes over to this stack of mail, picks up the envelope on top and comes walking toward me with her hand extended.

"You need to do something with this." She said with a smile.

"What is it?" I asked.

"Open it."

Hum…my name, her old address. Really odd…

I opened the envelope, and behold: it's an annuity of some sort. Says it's worth $1200, which is sure more than my first fruits check!

Now, this is gonna be a little difficult for you to get your mind around, but forget your thought process and *use your heart*, okay?

Like to told you, I have never had a 401K or any other kind of investment until I went to work for a laboratory in 2000, and when I left California to come back to Missouri in 2002, I cashed it out 'cause at the time there was nothing I could roll it over into, and it really wasn't worth much anyway. Check this out, the start date on this annuity that I'm suddenly holding in my hand is 1997. I didn't go out to work in California until 1998.

Are you gettin' a hold of this? I know it probably sounds so far fetched but hey, I really do have much better things to do with my evening than sit here and fabricate some outrageous tale! Meditate on what I've written here. Let it roll around in your heart. It should bring confidence! An immoveable, determined confidence and a great encouragement that *God takes care of His own*!

Hum...how to end this. I could really get on a roll! Maybe you've asked the LORD for some information on first fruits, and this is your answer! What fun!

Remember, God cannot be out-generoused and you cannot out-give the LORD. Everything you have to give, you have because He gave it to you. He knows your needs and your timeline. He has people all lined out to walk into your life at the "appointed time" for you to either be blessed by or for you to bless. It's so simple.

Tax money in fishes' mouths and annuities out of nowhere? Seems like it's just business as usual for God. Hum…and…should you find a penny in the street? Remember…it did fall from somewhere. :)

*I*t's been well over twenty years since I found the LORD and became a Christian. I'm one of those 'fanatics' who just pulled out all of the stops and decided that if the Word said I could do it, then I could do it, and if the Word said something was mine, then accurately following certain spiritual laws, it would most certainly be mine. Smile.

I've been through all kinds of stages and you know what I've found? No matter how long you've been walkin' with the LORD, if you're smart, you'll always remain a baby—and that's truly a good thing, 'cause babies and little children are teachable, trainable, and trusting. All of those attributes make for a very successful walk of faith.

Now then, my purpose here is not to preach. Pointin' and blabbin.' No. The purpose is to share with you one small event in my life in which believing God, resting in His goodness, and watching the remarkable effects of scripture when put to the test, produced exactly as the LORD promised it all would. It has all made for a very pleasant, fun, and most remarkable story: "Little Blacky."

So rest with me for a moment. And as we visit, open your heart to the fact that God has nothin' but very good things planned for you, and when He had David write the promise in Psalms 37:4 that if you delight in Him, He will give you the desires of your heart, that's *exactly* what He meant.

Little Blacky

"I will never buy a black car," and *"I will never buy a Corvette."*

I cannot even begin to tell you how many times I said those exact words over the past several years. But how many of you know that "never" always has an uncanny way of comin' back to bite ya in a most inconvenient place? Can ya say, "Amen?"

Sittin' here with a big grin on my face, 'cause this actually *is* a story about a Corvette.

I've always been a car buff. I got that from my dad. We had really nice cars. Some of them on the unique side, but unique back then is kind of common place now. Corvette was never even a thought for me. Not really sure why….guess 'cause when they were first born, seems everyone made such a huge fuss about them, when a Jaguar XKE, to me anyway, was really a far more classy, pretty car.

Corvette also seemed to be geared toward men. Men always looked better in a Corvette than a gal. The times I remember seein' a woman in a Corvette, she was pretty much a cigarette-smokin,' bleached-blonde, almost a biker-lookin' chick. So, the whole ambience of Corvette was never a draw for me at all. Sure, I've watched 'em change over the decades. They've grown up to be sleek and pretty. Don't know what you'd want that kind of power for when the speed limit is seventy. Nothin' but a major temptation if ya ask me. Besides, I'd never buy a Corvette.

I'll never forget the day shortly after I started work at Columbia Regional Hospital Laboratory in 2002. I was introduced to Dr. Chadwick Linder, MD. Tall, friendly, really likable young man, the kind of a person any parent would be proud to have as their son. We hit it off but quick when we had our first conversation about cars…oh yeah. From that day forward, we *always* had something to talk about and believe me, we did! He would talk to me about his Corvette, and I'd share stuff about Laddie, my gunmetal gray 1986 Nissan 300 ZX. We talked a lot about cars.

> If you ask anything in my name, I will do it.
>
> John 14:14

> If you abide in me, and my words abide in you, you shall ask what you will and it shall be done unto you.
>
> John 15:5

> Until now, you have asked nothing in my name. Ask and you will receive, that your joy may be full.
>
> John 16:24

Then came... "The Day."

I was working the weekend, and Dr. Linder was on call. He was makin' his rounds and dropped by to see how things were goin.' 'Course we started talkin' our usual fun line of conversation, and he got this sudden grin on his face as he said, "I brought my Corvette today, you wanna come see it?"

Well…I sat there thinking, "A Corvette…sigh…gee…he's such a nice kid…it's not very often that a guy his age would even be interested in spending time with someone old enough to be his mom. He seems to be real proud of his car."

Guess there was a small time warp as I sat there thinkin' and maybe he was beginning to feel like "the jury's been out too long here" so he added, "It's right out in the doctors' parking lot."

I nodded. "Sure, it's kind of quiet right now. Let's go."

So, off we went towards the doctors' parking lot. Down a couple of hallways, up some stairs and through another hallway to the door. 'Course, Dr. Linder is makin' lots of pleasant chatter about the Corvette and stridin' along with those long legs of his. I was doin' my double-time best to keep pace with him as we walked and was also feelin' a bit honored that he would take the time to share with me.

Through the back door. It was the weekend, so there was next to no one in the lot…except…this little...very shiny...black...*totally striking* Corvette. When I saw her, it was like...well, I don't know. Suddenly I was standin' there lookin' at the most beautiful little car I had ever seen. And it wasn't like, "Wow, look at that car!" No. It came sighin' out of my heart, "Wooooooow, loooook at thaaaat caaaar!"

By this time, Dr. Linder is just blabbin' *huge*, and I wasn't hearin' a word he was sayin'! I was just...*overcome* with this *car*! He opened the driver's side door, and this smell of leather came waftin' out at me! Just about laid me out!

I got the Grand Tour! Showin' me this, and pointin' out that. I'm walkin' around her just takin' her all in. 1985 Z51. *No* swirl marks in her paint (any automobile aficionado will tell you those are the absolute *bane* of the black car owner). Precious few marks on her. Chamois buff colored leather inside. Just pristine! Never been out in the rain, little eyes open and close when ya turn her lights on and off, and one very elite identifying mark: a decal in the middle of her windshield with "Medical" written on it. It was put on her when Dr. Linder and his brother were allowed to take her on the infield of the Indy 500 one year. And are ya sittin' down? *Less than 50,000 miles on her!* Who could ask for anything more perfect! Hence the very trite, redundant but totally *exact* description of a name: Black Beauty.

I was not ready for this! I finally open my mouth, and you know what comes out? Check this out! This is *totally* bizarre! "Dr. Linder, I'll tell you what. If you ever decide to sell this car, I'd like to be first in line to buy her." (Yes, I really *did* say that! *It's true!*)

He very respectfully, and with no apology (that's the way he is—you always know where you're at with him, and I like that a lot) told me that his dad was for sure first in line and he was going to have to honor that, but if he was ready to sell her and his dad didn't want her, then I could be first in line. Sounded more than fair to me.

"Okay..." I thought, but you know what? (Smilin' as I write here.) Dr. Linder left to check on another hospital, and as I was walkin' back to the lab alone through those hallways, I found myself actually askin' God for her. Yeah, I prayed to be able to have her. Sure did.

Guess it was about two weeks later, Dr. Linder came to work and announced to me that he *was not* going to sell Black Beauty to his dad 'cause the man lives on a dirt road and besides the obvious cosmetic factors, there was the roughness of the road that would be real hard on Blacky. I was suddenly *first in line*!

Way to go, God!

> Have faith in God. For surely I say unto you, whosoever shall say to this mountain "be thou removed and be cast into the sea," and shall not doubt in his heart but believes those things that he says will come to pass, he shall have whatsoever he says.
>
> Mark 11:22–23

> ... Even God, who quickens the dead and calls things that be not as though they were.
>
> Romans 4:17

Now mind you, this was not gonna come to pass right away. Dr. Linder was not ready to sell her but he would occasionally say in a most confidential way, "I've been looking at other women" (meaning cars). He would come get me with an invitation to his office where he'd have the 'Dream of the Day' on his computer for me to see. They were mostly Corvettes. Oh my, and when his brother bought a *new* Corvette? My stars, he really had the fever! And the most fun part about it? Whenever we'd see each other around work whether there were others around or not, we would always talk very seriously about how *I* had this Corvette that *I* was letting him borrow! We almost always spoke of her as being mine. *I* was letting him drive *my* car. The fun, *very* expensive day was when he came into my work area and announced to everyone there that he had just put *new tires* on *my car*!

> Commit your way to the LORD, trust also in Him and He shall bring it to pass.
>
> Psalm 37:5

Ya know, this went on for almost two years. I never got "car fever." Wasn't looking at other Corvettes. Never even asked Dr. Linder if he was sure he wanted to sell her to me. Gee, never even asked him *when* he'd sell her. It was just ongoing fun. Then came the day he stood at the door with that special smilin' look he gets when he's fixin' to say something to capture my attention and said, "I'm gonna buy a Mustang."

"*I beg your pardon?*" 'Bout fell out of my chair! "A Mustang, Dr. Linder? *A Mustang*?" For sure my voice went up a couple of octaves. "Son? *Have you lost your mind?* Where did all of this come from?"

Welp, he started into this dissertation that he'd seen the new Mustang and followed with this litany of all that it had on it—just this massive fount of information. "Dr. Linder, if you were talkin' to me about a horse, I'd be real excited for ya but no, there's a huge prob here!"

"What's that?" he asked, already widely smilin' and just waitin' for the answer.

"This thing has *Ford* written on it!"

Course we were all smiles with sporadic laughter as we teased back and forth a little more, but I'll tell ya, I had known the guy long enough to understand that he wasn't just jokin' here. *He was gonna buy a Mustang!* Good gravy, and when his *other* brother bought one, the boy was *on fire*! It *had* to be blue with all of this extra trash on it. Just like his brother's.

Another..."The Day"

Here comes Chad Linder goin' Mach III with his hair on fire! A boy and his machines on a mission, tellin' me that he'd done all of his homework on the internet and knew *exactly* what he wanted. He had called the local Ford dealership in Columbia, and they said they'd have to order it. However, he also called the dealership in Jefferson City (about thirty minutes away). "I called Kehoe in Jeff and asked if they had a 2006 Vista Blue Mustang GT. When they said yes, I told 'em I'd *take it*!"

If you could have heard his voice and seen his face! The boy was serious! He had just bought it sight unseen over the telephone. He also added that the salesman probably thinks he was just jerkin' him around when he said he'd take it. But that he sure was gonna "*Take it!*"

Hum...seems like the ball was suddenly in my court. Had ample opportunity to shop for a loan the following day, and even though my credit is absolutely sterling, not even the bank that loaned me the money for Blondie, my 2002 Toyota pickup, would give me a good rate cause Blacky was so old. Hey, and believe me, Dr. Linder was giving me a very good price on her. It was suddenly lookin' kind of bleak.

But ya know, God has His way of just turnin' up when you think all is lost and nothin's gonna work. It was the loan officer who offered the information that I had just paid off Blondie and suggested that I use her for collateral! Silly person that I am, I had no idea how much I still owed on her. I always just paid $100 extra a month. Just figured they'd notify me when she was paid for. Almost couldn't believe it when the loan officer told me Blondie was free and clear. He had actually *just that day* put her title in the mail to me. Amazing timing.

And now, for one of my most favorite scriptures of all time. It is written sixty-five times in the New Testament and most certainly deserves a drum roll:

And it came to pass.

The actual, real live, *goin' down in history…* *"THE DAY"*

And oh, what a day it was—more like I had just walked into a dream. Couldn't have had a more beautiful day! Dr. Linder and I drove Blacky down to Jefferson City (yeah, I got to drive).

We did the bank thing, I wrote him a check for Blacky, and then we went to the Ford dealership. They had the blue Mustang sittin' right out in front all by itself, and I parked Blacky a couple of parking places away.

There they were together. Odd kind of picture, really: Blacky…Mustang…

Blacky…

Mustang.

Blacky…

a…

Mustang.

There just was *no* comparison. Well, the way I was lookin' at them, that is.

'Course the salesman was out in that lot *so fast*! He was walkin' toward us just talkin' away with a huge smile on his face and hand extended from the moment he broke through the show room doors. Entertaining, really. I'll bet this was the only car he'd ever sold that he didn't even have to sell!

'Course he shook Dr. Linder's hand first, introduced himself (just about fallin' down thrilled!), and then asked Dr. Linder, "Is this your wife?"

We answered in unison, "No, she's—I'm—a friend." And the strangest thing happened: our answer didn't seem to stick at all! The salesman showed us inside to the gal who was gonna do all of the paperwork, introduced Dr. Linder and then introduced me as his wife!

For a brief moment Dr. Linder and I must have looked somewhat like identical twins both lookin' at each other with the same expression and both getting the revelation that it was probably pretty useless at this point to even try reminding the salesman that we weren't married; besides, I was suddenly havin' the time of my life! Hey, it isn't every day that a little ole garden variety shredder like me gets to buy a Corvette and be married to a tall, good lookin' doctor, ya know? All in the same day!

And I'll tell you what, I *remained* his wife all through the paperwork process and on into meetin' the fellas in the parts department and the folks in the body shop. Just so proud!

Well, Chad Linder sure did buy himself a Mustang. Sigh…and ya know, guess it hadn't really hit me at all, even when I was drivin' Blacky home, finally flyin' solo. Just stylin' along…shades on, cuddled down into her so comfy seat….listenin' to the rumbley purr of her engine…seein' the reflection of the trees, sky, and clouds on her hood…favorite worship CD just a playin' away. What a time.

So, Little Miss "I'll *never* buy a black car, and I'll for sure *never* buy a Corvette" had finally come out on the other side of never, and what thrill it has been.

Me and Blacky have great fun together. The little gal turns heads. Oh my, and there was the day this young fella came across two service bays at the gas station just to tell me how pretty he thought Blacky was. The memory makes me smile. Wow, and have I ever learned about washin' a black car! The agony of doing it and the *ecstasy* when you're done!

'Course, I occasionally do still tease Dr. Linder that his horse has "Ford" written on it but Dr. Birkby, our Medical Director, is usually standing within earshot and comes to Dr. Linder's rescue by loudly reminding me that I *"bought a plastic car!"*

Dr. Linder and I are the best of friends and now, there's a special kind of bond we share 'cause of Blacky. It's a "family thing." He knows that she's still part his.

A most precious addendum to this story is that Dr. Linder donated a portion of Blacky's proceeds to the Children's Ministry at his church. He's very much enjoyin' his iron horse and the fact that his family fits into it, but I know...there's just a "knowing"...that one of these days, he'll buy another Corvette.

Dr. Linder, Little Blacky and me.

It's the Little Things

A few weeks ago, I was scheduled to work the weekend, so I had the Thursday before the weekend off. I left work Wednesday afternoon determined to do some shopping at a very popular retail/grocery store so that I would have no needs to attend to on Thursday. The day would be free and clear.

So there I am was, Wednesday evening, just draggin' myself along through the store, and I came upon these light cotton summer blouses. Real cute and only $10. I chose a yellow one.

I was in the check out, and the cashier was very friendly. She and I were chattering along about how beautiful the weather was. She came to the blouse, remarked how cute it was, and also asked me if I wanted the hanger, which I gladly accepted.

Odd thing, I had left there real excited to get home so I could try on the blouse and when I got home, I got all involved in putting everything away and playing with my cats, and I forgot all about the blouse.

It was way later when it dawned on me that I didn't remember seein' the blouse. Didn't remember putting it in the car either. Yep, I had left it at the store. Crumb! I sure wasn't gonna go back there right then and immediately started this non-stop raggin' on myself to the LORD. "Daddy, that was sooo stupid of me! Here I am over there so I don't have to go tomorrow and drat!" Rag, rag, rag. "The very last thing I wanted to do was go over there again" Blah-blah-blah. But then I reminded myself that I had a breakfast date for Thursday morning with a most celebrated friend, and the restaurant was in the same huge parking lot as the retail store. Good plan. Breakfast and then go see about the blouse after. Okay, I was better.

With that decision came the thought that I needed to be sure I had the sales slip, and when I found it in my wallet, the loving warmth of the LORD came over me. There, half way down the sales slip was the charge for the blouse *twice*. The checker had charged me for it two times, and hey, *if I hadn't left the blouse there, I never would have known about the double charge.*

When I got to the store after breakfast, it was so early there was only one person in the customer service line instead of the usual twenty, and the exchange was totally easy. I got my blouse, and the customer service representative gladly put the $10 bill from the overcharge into my hand.

I never would have known. To me, this is a remarkable witness that the LORD has very subtle and fun ways of reminding you that He's with you. That sure was the feeling I got when I looked at the charge slip and saw the error. I could hear Him softly say, "I'm here." The Man who worked mighty miracles while He was here on this earth, who rose from the dead so that *you* can believe in mountain-moving miracles in your life does, in fact, take pleasure in the little things.

You Can't Do That! 'Cause You're a Girl! That's Why!

Can't even begin to tell ya how many times I heard that growin' up. Please. See, and all it did was just make me want to try harder to play guy-type sports. I remember in high school, I used to dream about playin' football! It's true. Of course I was the quarterback! You gotta a prob with that?

I was a real tomboy. Used to just *drive* my mom! She was from Boston and had these grandiose ideas of sendin' me to finishing school, boarding school, charm school, dear LORD, just *anything* to make a lady out of me!

Somewhere between high school and college, I did become a lady. A little rough around the edges but little by little, yeah...a lady. Not all prissed out or nothin.' No. I did start becomin' aware of how I looked, and my clothes had to be just so, but still all of my good friends were guys. I could hang.

Then came college. I went to Marymount College, an all-girls school. At the time it was located in Palos Verdes, California, directly up the hill from what was then Marineland. That was a *long* time ago.

This school was filled with the elite chicks. Some actually from Europe, but most from the East coast. Lotta wealth, sass, explosive temperaments, egos as big as Lake Michigan. Basically just a bunch of spoiled brats. I didn't want to hang.

During my first two years at Marymount the "tomboyness" just kind of dripped off of me. 'Course my mom was thrilled. I even learned how to play bridge. But ya know what? I was still me on the inside. Car fanatic, loved horses, loved to fish, massively enjoyed the car races, the demolition derby, hey, and Roller Derby! Shirley Hardman, Ralphy Valadarez, John Long, Chucho Rodriguez, and Al Fabuloso! *Roller Derby! Yes!*

I was a total boxing fanatic, but never got into hockey, and I also never lost the attitude that if a guy can do it, then I can do it! And I don't mean stupid stuff like lifting 300 pounds and bein' just asinine macho. Nah.

All of my college years were spent doin' a very serious pre-med thing. I graduated with a BS in Biology. From there my whole life was medicine. The tomboy had turned into a medical technologist. None of the rest of that junk seemed to matter any more. Sure I could still hang, but hey, I found myself with a husband in Vietnam and having to make a living. Whole 'nother story. The years just drifted on by.

A long ways down the road, in 1982, this totally marvelous thing happened to me: I found the LORD and got saved. Praise God for that. He truly turned my life around and into something worth living. To say "God is good" is a flamin' understatement. This is not just a paragraph stuck in at the end of page one, either. Now, I happily confess that without Him I am *nothing* and can do *nothing*. I am who I am because of Him and no one or anything else. I am so, *so* grateful. And now you can hear the rest of this story.

One of the greatest learning experiences I ever had was when I went back to California in 1998 after living in Missouri for almost twelve years to set up a crime scene cleaning department for my cousin's janitorial and building maintenance company.

The very first thing I learned was a whole new spin on the word "clean." I was being taught by the very best. My cousin had a phenomenal crew—all Hispanic, mostly from Guatemala—and they were workers extraordinaire! I learned how to clean in a way my dear mom never even had a clue about. Learned finite touches on detailing. My cousin had done a lot of restoration. She and I worked closely, and oh my, did I ever learn about how to *really* paint something. Not this "over dirt" trash. No! And finishing woodwork? Oh my, two coats of primer and then *at least* two coats of semi-gloss with light sanding in between coats. Oh, yeah. Just a satin finish.

And smilin' back on it now as I write, it was the LORD preparing me for the "money pit" house I was gonna buy when I came back to Missouri in 2002. Hang on to your hat now.

Yeah, I bought it, literally. The house was built in 1940. Mortared stone exterior. Just a beautiful little place in a historical neighborhood. The plus was it had a new roof the year before, and a nice upgrade in the kitchen. The original hardwood floors were just beautifully kept. There was something so solid about the place, and it had such a lovely feel about it. The first time I walked in it just felt like home.

Little by little I started actually seeing what I had bought. Windows just in sorry shape. Hey, and these weren't just regular windows, either. No, they all had to be special order 'cause the stone openings were all different sizes. The upstairs bathroom was…oh…used, and that's putting it mildly. The fact that it had the original *lavender* tub, pedestal sink, and toilet was actually kind of fun until you started really lookin' at 'em. Yeah, for real, lavender.

I was gonna have to do something with it. There was also the most bizarre paneling I'd ever seen in the add-on den. It was a natural wood with multiple very generous coats of 1940s orange shellac that actually did look brown. I didn't realize how penetrating it was till I tried to paint over it. Five or six coats of KILZ and it was still bleedin' through brown! In short, everywhere I looked there was something, and the bottom line was *huge time and money*!

The real cold shot came when I realized the sellers had lied on the disclosure about a few things, and I was lookin' at more money than I could ever have imagined.

I will tell you this: in a most miraculous way, suddenly (I love God's "suddenlys") I had two real fine young men walk into my life who just happened to be lookin' to pick up some extra money. They knew how to do all sorts of handy man and remodeling type stuff. They also came at a more than reasonable price. I never could have afforded the things that were done had I not had those boys. Couldn't have been more blessed. Rick and Ryan, my Two Rs.

Those boys…The things they accomplished in one year. That bathroom remodel was a *phenomenon*. They took it all the way down to the frame work.

Did new electrical wiring, new plumbing. It took a while too. That's also when we found out what the little house was made of on the inside. The walls were actually redwood slats with cement poured into them and then shored up with real thick brick tiles. I like to say it like this: Jesus will have come and gone but 1936 Hayselton will still be standing!

Boy howdy, did I ever paint and paper. The boys also did lots of crown molding and chair rail. Wow and wow. I couldn't believe how lovely it was coming out—just as pretty as a picture. I did a ton of cosmetic plastering of small cracks. The place was actually lookin' almost brand new.

Now then, I brought you all this way to tell ya about one very special thing that happened to me in that house. In the living room there was this very narrow, tall closet. It had seven shelves that were 12" by 24" and about 1 ½ thick, and some of 'em were warped. Odd thing is they came out kind of easy, but woe to the person who was gonna paint them and then put them back in again! Seems that just happened to be me.

This was gonna be the finishing touch on that little house. All I had left to do was "that" closet.

The boys still had all of their tools there. Rick had just finished the chair rail in the living room, and ya know what? His miter saw was sittin' right there on the living room floor not fifteen feet from where I was working.

I look back on this, shake my head, and laugh at myself. I finally got all of those shelves out and was getting them painted. The trial came when it was time to get them back into the closet, and I'll be switched, seems none of 'em wanted to fit! I had numbered them so I knew which one went where, but I guess the paint swelled them a little? Don't know. All I did know was they sure *did not* fit any more! *Drat!*

So, what did I have at my disposal? My little 'mouse' sander (love that little guy) and some pretty heavy duty files and a plane that I had used on a few of the doors, oh yeah, and a little dremel.

Rick's saw is sittin' right there.

I sanded, and sanded, and sanded. Goin' in and out of that closet *untold* times tryin' to get those shelves to fit, and it didn't seem to be makin' a hill of beans' difference. It really didn't look like it was gonna take that much and I have no idea what those shelves were made of, but it was like they were petrified! I was just *sweatin' bullets* goin' in and out of that closet!

Rick's saw is *still* just sittin' there.

The plane and the dremel were literally bouncing off the wood and you can flat out forget the whole file foray.

Now I'm *lookin'* at Rick's saw!

I'm tellin' ya right now that thing was laughin' at me! What was surprising about it is evidently I really had become all lady-fied. I was thinking about how the thing is just *so noisy* and how *that blade* is *so dangerous*, "Penny, guys have lost fingers and hands with those things!"

Little smart alec saw just sittin' there lookin' all smug and in control. What it was actually doin' was sittin' there smirkin,' *"You can't use me caaaaause yurrrrr aaaa girl!"*

Then I suddenly could feel it risin' up in me, *"Ooooh yeah? If Rick can do it, I can do it!"* Said it out loud with *great conviction* as I walked on over to it and knelt down in front of it. I was movin' *very slowly* just in case it was gonna suddenly turn itself on and scare the sap out of me. It was already glarin' real mean at me, tryin' to run me off. Miserable little twit saw!

I wrapped my fingers around the blade guide handle and moved it up and down, watchin' how the plastic shield rolled away as the blade lowered. "Okay, that's good," I thought. I also noticed these little built-in buttons on either side of the handle that evidently would turn the saw on. Practiced pushin' the buttons while gradually lowering the blade just to get the feel of 'em. I'm moving real slowly and just taking it all in. Next thing, of course was to plug the little guy in.

The racket was unsettling at first and yeah, the power surge is pretty impressive when the blade is first engaged, but long story short, it didn't take long to get the hang of it and I was on a roll! It took me about fifteen minutes to do what I had been struggling with for a whole day! Feelin' *so* empowered! *Don't mess with me!*

That day I faced off with that saw truly opened a huge door for me. If I had let that thing bully and intimidate me into thinkin' that I couldn't use it, oh, what I would have missed!

Since that day, I bought another home and have done a ton of my own remodeling. I bought my *own* laser miter saw and have put in new fancy baseboards, chair rail, molding and even did the "all the rage" picture frame accents on the walls. I've framed out doors and windows. It has come out just terrific.

My latest accomplishment is actually laying porcelain tile in the foyer. Fifty square feet and I used three different sizes of tile to create a pattern. Got a trusty little wet saw and we just did fabulous together. It is beautiful! A marble countertop in the guest bath is next!

So…I can't do *what*?

Whaaat?

Don't tell me I can't do that!

Yes! I! Can!

'Caaause I'm aaa girl! That's why!

Life around the Lake

I used to live in the loveliest place on earth. It was Lake Champetra, and for those who actually knew about it, the mention of it was, "Oh yeah, that's out there past the gravel pit on 63 just before you get to Hartsburg." Yep, that's where it is alright. But most people would just look at ya. "Lake what? Where's that?"

That lake had to have been the best kept secret in all of Mid-Missouri. It was also my gift from the LORD. Coming from California, it was more like a vacation spot than a home. A place you'd only dream about living. Back in 1987, there were probably only thirty-five, maybe forty homes around that lake. Big ole beautiful lake, too. Spring fed. It was my first home in Missouri. I came from LA, nothing but concrete and steel, to the most lush, indescribably beautiful place I'd ever seen. There are times I sure do miss the place.

Now you must know that all of this loveliness was not without its challenges, the most outstanding of which was the Lake Champetra road. The lake sits a little over a half-mile deep into a valley, and to get into that valley, you'd have to travel this steep, very winding road.

During the summertime, that was not a problem at all, but the winters in Mid-Missouri sometimes are to be dealt with, the ice especially. There were several times I'd leave work at 11:30 p.m., and if it had been snowing, it would take about a half hour just to get home. Drivin' much slower than usual, and in the dark. Man, and I'll tell ya, you really lose sight of how *dark* it really does get when there are no street lights and the cloud cover is blocking the moon and the stars. I would stop at the crest of the Champetra hill, gather myself mentally and start praying before starting the descent. The wind would just *whip* along through the top of that hill! It was always icy after a snow.

I will tell you right now, driving that road late on a winter's night all by yourself was not for the fainthearted. It's actually just an extra-wide one-lane road and you really had to be an accomplished snow and ice driver. What's bad is you can have all of the experience on winter roads possible, but a road that has two inches of snow and ice underneath, hairpin turns, and some stretches as steep as forty-five degrees can be full of surprises. I never took that road casually during the winter time. If there was no visible snow, there could be the dreaded black ice. You can kiss it goodbye on that stuff!

I've been a faithful believer in God, the LORD Jesus, the Holy Spirit, and angels for some time now. During the times I would be traveling that road on winter nights alone, I had great evidence of their existence in my life. Boy, there was one night...

It was mid-winter and just as *cold*! *Gosh!* The weather was the big buzz at work all day and evening. We had a snow storm come into the area and stall. I mean that thing just *sat down* on our little town, and it snowed and snowed and *snowed*! There was a big prob too 'cause it brought sleet and ice with it. The roads were a mess and the later it got, the colder it got. Sigh…the drive home…'Course I could have stayed at the hospital where I worked but when you've just worked two sixteen-hour shifts back to back, and it's time to go, it's time to *go*!

I got all bundled up like a toad (could hardly move), walked outside, and still just got *slapped* around by that cold, whippin' wind. It wasn't very far to Boy Truck, my little four-wheel-drive Nissan. Seems like it took forever for the little guy to warm up. It was still lightly snowing, a remarkably beautiful sight. The snowflakes were capturing the parking lot lights and just sparkling like little stars.

So, off we went towards home. The road crews had really been out doing a fabulous job. The streets were a little dicey, but Highway 63 was real doable. I went thirty-five miles per hour all the way home, took my exit turn, and started up the hill toward the Champetra turn off.

Odd, I didn't actually realize that I'd already been prayin' in the spirit on the way home until I got within eye-shot of the Champetra turn-off sign and suddenly started prayin' louder. Yeah, the fear was tryin' to come.

Pulled right up to the turn-off, took Boy Truck out of gear, started whisperin' the name of Jesus, and started down the hill at a crawl. I don't even think I was doin' one mile an hour. I would roll a few feet and then very gently brake to see how the tires would grab. Don't know why, I just always did it that way, and just 'cause they grabbed well in one place sure didn't mean they'd grab well in others!

I was less than a hundred feet down the hill when I see this…this….*apparition*, for lack of a better word. It was over to the left about fifteen or twenty yards off the road into the forest. This huge, twisted wreckage of something. Between the darkness and my headlights creating real bizarre reflections, this was suddenly lookin' like I had driven right into a Stephen King movie! I'm serious! Never seen anything like it. Hey, and whatever this enormous piece of machinery was, it came to rest on its back with its tires in the air! That I *could* see!

'Course seein' this just created an even greater sense of danger. I was prayin' along, heart just a beatin,' and barely movin' down the hill.

Finally I'm at the bottom of the hill and make my left onto North Shore Drive. I was feelin' somewhat relieved but still had a ways to go yet. After the turn, you head down a little hill that's very steep, and infamously icy during winter. Then from there you had a double whammy: the big lake on the right and the estuary (more lake) on the left. There was no ditch, just water on both sides of the road. This went for about a hundred yards and then the final challenge: a small but steep hill with a sharp hairpin turn at the top. Jim Roberts's house sat right there. We used to call it Roberts Hill. I lived in the house next to his. By the time I finally got to that hill, with Boy Truck in four-wheel drive, we took it like a couple of little storm troopers.

I must have lost ten pounds that night just drivin' home but, oh, the feeling when I walked through my front door! The radiating heat from the earth stove, my wonderful little cats waiting for me. Home. Thank you, LORD!

Ya know what made the front page of the Jefferson City Tribune the next morning and with a most rare *color* picture to boot?

That wreckage was actually the Hartsburg Volunteer Fire Department Truck! *For real!* I just saw the picture from a distance and didn't have time to stop and read the article. No one I talked to that day had any idea of what happened. No one's house at Champetra caught fire. Hey, and if they were doing some kind of a drill? Hum...Real puzzlement. That was *so* bizarre!

I lived out at Lake Champetra for ten years and never put Boy Truck in the ditch. Now, there was one day we sure did do a 360 on Roberts Hill in the ice. Got spun around real good. That storm went for a whole day and night, leaving at least and inch and a quarter of ice on everything. I'm sure it was thicker in certain places on the road. It was so bad the cinder/sand truck had to *back down* the hill into the lake area! We were all iced in for two days!

Sittin' here smiling and rememberin.' You know, there was a resident who just couldn't seem to get the hang of drivin' in and out of there.

A usual winter's evening, I crest the hill and start down and here in the ditch over to the right was this champagne pink Infiniti. Never seen it before. Pretty little thing. Just *way* in the ditch. Checked real close to be sure there was no one in the car and continued easin' my way home.

Couple of nights later I'm driving in, and get to the bottom of the hill and here, literally engulfed in this huge bush, was this same Infiniti! Evidently just lost it on the hill and couldn't regain to negotiate the North and South Shore turns. All I could see was the poor little thing's backside hangin' out of the bush.

And then, very shortly after that (like within days), I was leaving the house to head into town one afternoon, got to Roberts Hill and here is that dear little Infiniti. You'd better believe I felt sorry for it by then! This time, she obviously had been lofted off the hairpin turn *high enough* to clear this section of barbed wire fence down the hill, and was literally stickin' up like a dart in the ditch! It was amazing!

And you know what?

I never saw that car again.

Life around the lake sure had its moments. There are times I look back on all of it and wonder how on earth I made it through those years. There are also times I miss that place and all of its restful beauty so very much. But things change. People change. God opens new doors. And in finale, there's only one way to go in life: forward.

Last Week I Went to Hell

It was last week. Holy Week. I came home from work, went downstairs to work out and listen to my favorite preachers that I tape every morning. Now, there are times I certainly do not exercise in the afternoon, but I very rarely miss watching what I have taped that day.

This was a very special afternoon indeed, because one of the pastors was actually preaching/teaching on the reality of Hell—something that is very rarely touched upon, let alone taught. He really had it together. Lots of descriptive scriptures and just kind of telling it like it is. Interesting. He suddenly stopped and with a very serious sadness he tenderly said, "Watch this."

What followed was a video. I have no idea who made it or who starred in it or where it came from. Don't know. But what followed…

I have been present in churches where once a year there's a salvation presentation. One that comes vividly to mind is "Heaven's Gate and Hell's Flames," in which loved ones dying and being carried off by demonic forces are depicted. Of course this evokes tremendous feelings of loss. Separation from loved ones. Anybody who has experienced loss of someone they love—grief. I've sat and cried watching it. The whole separation thing. I have lost loved ones and friends…such sadness. I don't think there's any feeling that rivals it.

After these presentations, I've seen people rush to the altar call. There's always overwhelming emotion, and it seems also some discernable confusion that has kind of bothered me.

But that's not what this was.

The scene opens with a pretty young girl in an ambulance. She's obviously been in an accident. I'm sure you've encountered numerous scenes like this on TV. There's blood on her face, but not enough to cover how pretty she is. Her neck is stabilized. There's the serious diligence of the two paramedics who are working on her. Lots of tubes. You can hear the beeping monitors in the background tracking out her vitals and heartbeat. She's very well aware that she's been badly hurt. She's scared and confused.

Suddenly, you hear the monitor flat line. Her eyes are open. She hears it too. You see the "knowing" in her eyes that she's dying. She *knows*.

The scene blackens and reopens. It's very shadowy and dark with smoke and intermittent flames in the background. You see her. The blood splatters are gone from her face. Her skin is sheet white and clammy. She's got some kind of odd gag in her mouth. It appears to be made of metal and there are spikes along the edges. Her eyes startle open and you hear the chains she's bound in clink and rattle as she tries to move and can't.

Little by little the sounds around her become more recognizable as being anguished cries, moans, and desperate pleadings of suffering and torment. There are also distorted, muffled growls and words from the tormentors. All you see is her face, which defies description with what is to follow. Her eyes...

There comes a progression of scenes. She is dragged from scene to scene by her chains through what appears to be a series of tunnels. The sights and sounds are graphic and yet subtle because mostly what you see is the reflection and response in her eyes. She makes vain, wheezy gasps at screaming.

Some scenes depict demons and others suffering people, the likes of which I have never seen on film. Horror and fear of such intensity that I could barely stand to watch it, but I was *captured* because it was *so real*. I was there! As I sit here writing it's almost like reliving it all over again. It's actually bringing me to tears. There's no way I can describe it. Her eyes...the agonizing, *relentless* terror.

I wasn't very far into the experience when I heard myself softly, slowly, and repeatedly whisper, "Forever...forever...forever..." as the reality and weight of an eternal hell was imposing itself upon me. My heart was pounding, and I was actually becoming nauseated as it continued. That had to be the *longest, most uncomfortable* five or so minutes I've ever spent in my life. It seemed to go on and on and on. By the time that video was over, I was feeling broken, empty, wrung out, and exhausted. I can't even begin to imagine doing eternity there.

You must know that relief came when the scene blacks out and reopens with the girl having been revived by the paramedics. The gag was gone. She could finally scream.

There's some hard things here that I'm constrained to write.

First of all, this was not some Stephen King gruesome fantasy. It was not *Alien vs. Predator* or *Jason and Friday the 13th* part 15. It wasn't some warped Freddie Kruger, *Omen*, *Exorcist*, or that Snipes mess, *Blade*. No…no. This was an astounding portrait of *reality*. A *very real* place.

I was actually experiencing *fear*. Genuine, gut deep, raw *fear*. Why? You know, that's a really good question!

I'm sitting there watching this, and it was like I was actually there with her. Isn't that what act-ing is all about? To get you to feel what the actor is supposedly feeling? Well, *I was*, and it kind of took me back a little. Hey, and I'm a Christian and have been most surely saved over twenty-five years now. I made Jesus the LORD of my life, put my hands to the plow and have not looked back.

Okay, so where'd the fear come from? Was I simply just all caught up in the moment and extreme visual thing that was going on? One thing for sure: I was experiencing these horrible feelings of sadness and grief *for her* and realizing this is most assuredly a place I would never want anyone to go. *Ever!* Or, here's a hard thought. Was I fearful because I was doubting my own salvation? I have never experienced such a vivid portrayal of hell.

Perhaps it was a bit of both, which is a little hard for me to conceive of, but the bottom line here is *I'm so glad I'm not going there, and seeing that video has put a new meaning to the word evangelist on the inside of me!*

There are so many people who take that idea of eternity so lightly. They laugh it off while allowing demons and hell to be fanaticized to their children in a daily onslaught of TV, games, and books—even clothing. The whole idea is to present hell as one huge party. The deception is so great!

When Jesus was asked a question, He always started with the most important aspects of the answer first. "See that no man deceive you," was His number one immediate answer to the disciples' question about the signs of the end of the age.

If you are a Christian, please take it to heart that all of your faith, believing, and time spent in study, fasting, and prayer is *not in vain*! Your Heavenly Father sees in secret and will reward you openly!

Also as a Christian, the most important thing you can ever *realize* is that you should feel just like God feels about people going to hell. The Bible says He does not want one to be lost, and I'll sure tell you that video has ignited a fire of compassion in my heart for the lost.

Finally, as a Christian, the most important thing you can ever *do* is to perfect the love walk of Jesus so that people will see Him in you and want what you've got! *Amen!*

If you *have not* made Jesus Christ the LORD and Savior of your life, I must tell you that God had me to write this especially for you. There were so many other things I wanted to do today, but He had you on my heart. He loves you so much and sent His Son to die for you so you can spend eternity in a wonderful place called heaven with Him. Hell is a real place. The choice is yours. I beg...*implore* you, please don't let that happen to you. Please don't go.

Aaaaah Yes... the Cigarettes

I will tell you right now, there is nobody, and I mean *nobody* who enjoyed smoking more than I did. The taste. The smell. The rush. Shakin' my head at me!

Marlboro was my favorite brand all through high school and part of college. Yes, high school. Then, as smoking became less and less the thing to do, I switched to a real low tar and nicotine brand: Carlton 100s. They were a longer cigarette, so I thought I was gettin' more. See, and the joke is that there were little holes located between the filter and the actual cigarette. This was part of the lower tar and nicotine invention. The only way to get any taste out of them at all was to squeeze on 'em with your thumb and forefinger to cover those holes while you were takin' a drag. Looked like you were smokin' a joint. For you long-time saved, fluff-folded Christians, that's slang for a marijuana cigarette. If you're an ex-smoker or still smokin' you should be grinnin' pretty big by now 'cause you've done the same dumb thing.

Being that cigarettes are legal, you never realize how addicted you are till you try to quit. Same with booze. Besides, if you're living in the world's system and they say it's okay, then, hey, it's okay.

After I found the LORD (He reined me in, praise God!), it was seeking Him and learning the word that became the driving force of my life. Oh my, and I had such great teachers! I cut my teeth and grew up at the feet of Fred Price, Kenneth Copeland and Brother Jerry Savelle.

Kenneth, with his sense of humor telling' his cryin' stories about those cigarettes. How he'd be driving along and loudly declare his deliverance and freedom from them and throw them out the window. Next thing, he'd be walkin' along the highway lookin' for them. I would have been right out there with him too!

And Brother Jerry has a fun story about when some preacher had him to stomp his pack of Winston cigarettes in church and say out loud, "I will never smoke again!"

I would listen to those tapes over and over again, sayin' out loud, and in total agreement as they preached, "Yeah! Yeah!" just hoping that something would finally take or hit me in the heart. Gee, *anything*! Slap me upside the head! *Anything* so I'd finally be free from those vicious weeds for ever.

Did that happen? No.

Deliverance from alcohol came a year after I got saved. But the cigarettes? They were going to be a major stronghold. I can't even begin to count, let alone remember the times I tried to quit smoking over the years. Try to realize and understand that you're not going through anything different from anybody else who's addicted to nicotine. It's the same hard addiction as alcohol, but the difference is that you can't have too many cigarettes, lose your mental capacity, and do something mega-embarrassing with possibly devastating consequences.

I don't have to tell you the major draw back with cigarettes (besides the fact they are deliberate, slow suicide) is that you, your clothes, your house, your car, and anything else you have smell just *horrible*!

Oh boy, and I worked very hard at defrayin' all of that too. I got one of those smokeless ashtrays, and it actually did work pretty good. Changing the filter on the thing was a *huge* eye-opener! All of that tar-brown, goo, sludge! And that's what you're breathin' in like you can't live without it!

I only smoked in my nest and kept my clothes in a different part of the house so they wouldn't smell. And of course there was gum and mouth wash. I had a complete arsenal. Just all of it. There was only one problem: you know what was with me *all of the time* and just totally reeked? My Bible. But there was an answer to that one too. I kept my church Bible with my clothes and my study Bible in my nest.

Before church, the smoking lamp was out for at least two hours. Everyone wants to hug, ya know?

So, why was I hangin' on so *hard*? Sigh...I had always had a weight problem. It had blighted me all through my childhood, and high school was horrible. I wasn't terribly overweight, but I sure could have been. Easily. I controlled my diet like it was the only thing that mattered in life. The cigarettes were my diet pills and kept my weight at bay.

Then when I got saved and discovered prayer and fasting, the weight tumbled off of me. I was finally, after thirty-nine years, thin and looking like I had always wished, and prayed, and wanted to look. Svelte (smile). I went from a size fourteen to a size four in about a year. My clothes looked just lovely on me. I don't have to tell you what it's like when you're finally, after *years*, pleased with how you look. The thought of gaining it all back, which is always a threatening side effect of quitting smoking, was a deep fear that I just wasn't ready to face.

The second equally strong reason I was not lettin' go was the fact that I had quit so many times before, once for over two years. There really is something about losin' that particular battle. Your family especially. My mom would get that wounded look (it was actually a Catholic look) and I would feel *sooo guilty* and like *suuuch a failure*. Like you're not angry and disappointed enough with yourself? It all leaves such a heavy mark. Tragic, really. There were times I thought I just couldn't live through another event like quittin' and then pickin' up the cigarettes again, because that was *always* going to happen. Failure would *always* come. No...no.

I came to Jefferson City, Missouri, in 1987 and it was during a pre-employment physical that I got blessed by a very compassionate young man by the name of Dr. William Kimlinger.

When we were going through the history and physical questionnaire, he noticed that I had marked the "yes" answer by smoking cigarettes, and it launched us into what I thought was going to be the usual physician/patient conversation about the evils and physical effects of smoking. Boy was I ever wrong. Praise God.

I quickly and quietly answered his questions about tobacco usage just bracing for what was to come. Perhaps he could sense the sorrow on my face and in my voice. He listened. I can still see his face. There was a softness in his eyes and remarkable kindness in his voice as he said words that were of such great encouragement and consolation. I know as long as I live, I will never forget them or that moment. It might as well have been the LORD Himself speaking to me as he said, "Penny, you have got to understand that all of the times you've tried to quit smoking are just stepping stones. Don't give up. You'll get there."

Big tears welled up in my eyes. You talk about a "Word in Season."

Did I run home and make a bunch of high goal plans to quit smoking? No. But I can tell you this. One of the hardest things I had to live with as a smoker was gone: the condemnation. All of the quit/failure blame, guilt, and conviction was gone just because I could finally see with Dr. Kimlinger's very simple words that I wasn't at the *end*. No, I was *still at the beginning*. Oh my, and the reassurance that brought. So grateful. Glory to God.

There's a very integral part of this story that will be covered entirely in another writing. You need to know about the Tea. Scripture Tea. It's needful to tell you just a little about it right now.

For at least twenty years now I have used a product called Scripture Tea as a part of my daily word time. It's a very tasty tea, and it has a scripture imprinted on the tab. I'm about to give you an example of why I have my tea every morning without fail. If I travel, the one thing I'm for sure to take with me is the tea. It has become the most astounding communication from God. Well of course, it's His word! It's His own special way of giving me a daily little friendly nudge and sayin,' "I'm here."

Also very important about the Tea is that they are individually wrapped for freshness. There was a time they were cellophane sealed so you could see in, but the tab was turned facing the bag so you couldn't see what the scripture was. They're wrapped in a special moisture resistant paper now. Every day has always been a surprise.

I tape the tea tab into my journal and write the date in my bible at the scripture reference. Logging the date is most important. Plus I always read the whole chapter. You're about to get a very small revelation of the overwhelming influence and blessing my daily Scripture Tea has been to me over the years.

So, we are now going to go to June 12, 1990, and a morning that was so special. I was doing my

Bible study and prayer time, and my Scripture Tea for the day was 2 Corinthians 12:9. In verse 7, Paul is talking about this "thorn in the flesh," a messenger from Satan that was sent to buffet him. In verse 8, he writes that he had asked the LORD three times to get the thing off of him. Actually, "asked" is a little watered down. It's more like "begged." And then the LORD actually *said* to him—evidently Paul actually heard His voice—"My grace is sufficient for thee: for my strength is made perfect in weakness."

Smile. You know what I was hearing and feeling in my heart as I read that? The LORD was giving me the heads up to get myself prepared to quit smoking. It was time. Had I read that scripture before? Of course. Countless times, but have you noticed that you can read a scripture, get one meaning out of it, and then read it again a few weeks later or even the following day, and you see something entirely different? That's why it's called the Living Word. This is sure what I was seeing on that morning.

Was I suddenly scared? No. I just sat there lookin' at 2 Corinthians 12:9 with His grace being sufficient and knowing it sure had to do with quitting those cigarettes. *He* was telling me, and from there, He started showing me. He was right there with me. There was nothing to be afraid of.

Philippians 4 came into my heart, so I turned there to verse 13 to look at doing all things through Christ who strengthens me, and behold: a date was written at verse 13. It was 7–21–88, and even though it was an old date, it currently corresponded to being just 9 days away.

"Hum…it's a target date," I thought. "…yeah…"

He was giving me nine days to get my head and heart together. Pretty good lead time, actually, and you know what's remarkable about it? Knockin' off the cigarettes had not even been on my mind! Cute thing is that my mom's birthday was July 17, and I was already realizing that my quitting smoking was a birthday gift to her from God.

One thing I can always depend on the LORD for: He knows me *so* much better than I know myself. Through that nine days, as He was walking me toward the target date, without fail on a daily basis, He had scriptures for me to encourage and exhort me. He also gave me a "God Idea." He's so good, He only needs one *o*. Smile.

This "God Idea" was this new product that I'm fully persuaded He had made just for me. It's called Nicorette. A nicotine gum. I'm sure you've heard of it.

Was this preparation to fail? Good heavens, no! Please remember the Bible says that Jesus was tempted in all ways as we are but without sin (Hebrews 4:15), and people center up on the "without sin" and forget that He was, in fact, tempted *just like* we are. That is *so important*! If anybody could know what I had already been through and was fixin' to go through, it was *Him*! I immediately considered the Nicorette as a gift and preparation for success. I prayed about it and was real okay with it in my heart.

Perhaps you're thinkin' that using the Nicorette was nothin' but a cop out. Hey, God has put people and things very generously into this earth all for our help and good. He also knows better than anybody just how much your faith can take. If your faith isn't strong enough to believe for a healing, He *wants* you to go to the doctor. Just because you go to the doctor doesn't mean that your expectancy can't be in

God. One of my favorite preachers says, "If it wasn't for doctors, half the Christians would be dead."

There is nothing wrong with using the helps that God has given us. There are stages and levels of faith, and God knows just where you're at and just what you need. So many people *limit their own faith* by surmising or thinking that God is going to handle a situation or answer a prayer in a certain way. Then when it doesn't happen according to this air castle they've built up in their minds, here comes discouragement and the excuses, the most common of which is, "Well, I guess God just didn't want me to have that…"

We need to have faith and just let God be God. That's something He does incredibly well! Can ya say "amen"?

On the evening of July 20, 1990, I got off work and headed home. As I was lighting one of my very last cigarettes, the LORD gave me some wonderful instructions. When I got home and was smoking the last cigarette of my life before bed, I was to take one of my split oak logs (I heated exclusively with wood) and nail some cigarettes to it in the shape of a cross.

All the way home, listening to praise music, I realized I was celebrating salvation and deliverance from one of the most subtle and vicious weapons in Satan's arsenal instead of grieving the loss of a long time friend. There was no fear at all.

When I got home, I did exactly what the LORD instructed me to do. I chose a beautiful piece of split oak and very on purpose nailed five cigarettes to it in the form of a cross.

Odd thing, the cigarettes were not old at all, and yet as those little one-inch finishing nails pierced the paper wrapping, they kind of shattered the area just around the nail hole. I remember thinking, "They are so fragile, and yet have been so strong and demanding in my life."

I finished nailing and then sat the oak/cross in my nest, where I spend my time with the LORD, right under my picture of Jesus. It was at that moment that I finished smoking my last cigarette.

I did not scurry around cleaning all of the ash trays and putting all of my smoking junk away. I had spent nine days in the Word, shoring up my faith, and I was ready. I had the Nicorette and my cigarette cross sitting under my picture of Jesus that

I look straight ahead at when I'm sitting in my nest. Keepin' my eyes on Him. I was ready. I was good.

July 21, 1990, I got up in the morning, and the very first thing was to look at my tea tab. It brought this huge smile and feeling of being so looked out after and loved. The tea for that day was 2 Corinthians 12:9, the Scripture Tea that started the whole thing nine days ago, and here it is today. His grace *is* sufficient. You talk about a comfort and encouraging word from the LORD? Like when you absolutely *know* that you are right on target with what He has for you.

As I was enjoying my tea, it was then that I got instructions from the LORD regarding the use of the Nicorette. I would be allowed six pieces of gum a day, and if I had a stressful day and did seven or eight, then the following day I could only have four or five. Just six per day. Period.

Ya know what you say to that? "Yes, Sir!" And then at all cost you *do it*!

Sittin' here smilin' as I write. I did that whole six a day Nicorette thing for the better part of three years. Looking back on it, I'm fully persuaded that the LORD in His mercy gave me that gum so I could get rid of the hand to mouth thing that smokers do, and the biggie? So that I wouldn't gain a bunch of weight and get all discouraged and depressed like I had in the past. He was truly babying me along. It worked too.

Then came the big day. I can't remember when it was, but for sure it's logged into my journal somewhere. Don't even remember any circumstance that surrounded it. What I do remember was the LORD impressing me that it was time to put the Nicorette away. I was way over all of the ancillary smoking habits. It was time to finally face off with the nicotine.

I will tell you right now that I had three of the most grinding and physically uncomfortable days I have ever spent in my life. For real! Was I tempted to actually smoke? No. I'd been free from all of that for three years. I could remember Brother Jerry saying as clearly as if it was yesterday, "If I can just make it through these next three days, I will *never smoke again!*" Hearing his voice like that in my heart was *so real* that I decided to literally lean on what he said and his three days became *my* three days.

Now for the glory. It was just three days. Smile. Came through it with flyin' colors. That was twenty years ago.

Did I gain weight? Just a tick, but I fight that on an entirely different level now. With good diet and exercise (which you should do anyway), it stays off.

One kind of interesting thing, though. Cigarette smoke still smells very good to me. If I am in an open area where there's a person smoking and some of it wafts my way, I don't find it to be offensive at all. It doesn't evoke any memories. Odd, it doesn't even seem familiar. It just smells good, and then it's gone.

So there ya have it. Smile. I'm so glad I was obedient to the LORD and allowed Him to help me. He'll do the same for you too.

Seek Him, and don't be feelin' all condemned and worthless. Talk to Him about it. You *are not* alone. If you're born again, you have His Spirit dwelling in you to teach, guide, and comfort you. Let Him design your program. Listen for Him. He will give you the best thoughts, ideas, and instructions. He knows *exactly* what will work for you.

If you're not born again, be advised that you are totally missing out on all of the lovely, most fabulous things that "this life" (Acts: 5: 20) has to offer in Him and through Him.

Are you ready? Focus your attention and open your heart, okay?

Close your eyes and do your best to hear the voice of the LORD saying your name, and then follow with this: "...you have got to understand that all of the times you've tried to quit smoking are just stepping stones. Don't give up. You'll get there."

And Then ... God Gave Me a Sign

The year is 2002, March, long about the 11th day and my most treasured, faithful friend Elyse and I are moving me back to Missouri from the Los Angeles area.

We've been on the road for two days. I'm driving The Lad (a dashing, gunmetal grey Nissan 300 ZX, who I affectionately called Laddie), with all three of my cats on board. Elyse is piloting the big ole twenty-eight-foot truck we rented. Except for the hard winds through New Mexico which were actually blowin' the truck around the road a little, it's been an easy trip.

Usually I journal every day, but with the daily eight- to ten-hour drive, the bathtub and the bed beat the journal all to smithereens! This is one rare instance where God showed Himself in a most simple but strong way that is not logged into my journal that I can find anyway. I could have written about it the following week but the important thing is not what, how, or when it happened, but what God actually *did*. He brought it to mind a few days ago. It's a genuine Psalm 91 experience. The memory put a smile in my heart and a most comforting reminder that he cares so much about his children and is always lookin' out for us. I'm believing Him to help me tell this correctly.

The one thing I do remember quite clearly is we were somewhere between Joplin and Springfield, Missouri. There ain't nothin' between Joplin and Springfield! At least there wasn't back in 2002.

We're cruisin' along. It's a lovely, mild day and behold: here comes this noise from the right flank of Laddie. It started real subtly, but was getting consistently louder. Over a time span of what I'm remembering to be about an hour that noise went from being a little something that you really weren't sure you were actually hearing to ka-thunk, ka-thunk, ka-thunk! We were in trouble.

It had to be a tire. A tire! Out there in the middle of nowhere. A *tire*! Of course, I'm slowing waaaay down. Elyse is behind me, and I can see there's no obvious change in the look on her face.

Now then, there are times when I pray that I approach God with very quiet respect; an orderly and very on-purpose presentation with thanksgiving. But then there are times ya just need to talk to him, *stat*! I remember there was some fear tryin' to come on me, and I also remember *exactly* what I said, "Daddy, I'm needin' some help here. Thank ya, Sir."

Moments later, I had slowed to a crawl and had almost pulled all the way off onto the shoulder of the road (sittin' here smilin' as I write). Suddenly, as I live and breathe, here's this handwritten, make-shift *sign*. It's true! It's just layin' there kind of propped up and nestled into some larger tufts of grass. It's small, about three and a half feet square with a white background and black writing. What does it say? "Tires fixed here." It also had a straggly lookin' arrow which would indicate an off-ramp. And yeah, there was an off ramp!

Well, Laddie and I just ka-thunked very slowly up that off-ramp, *upon which you could only go one way* (God really does know how to show us which way to go), and we continued down this very narrow gravel road for about oh…a quarter mile, and ya know what's just sittin' right there? A bunch of old dead cars, piles of tattered, torn up used tires, and a pretty good sized corrugated metal building with new tires and a couple of service bays inside. Amazing.

I pulled in and this very countrified gentleman just came right on out to greet and meet. He was friendly and liked cats which to me was a huge confirmation. (Smile.)

Do you have any idea what went off in my heart when he walked around to Laddie's rear, took a quick look, and very seriously told me there was a huge bulge on the inside of the tire and had it blown while we were on the road, it would have literally torn that side of Laddie all the way off? I had to go sit down.

He put two brand new tires on Laddie's rear at a price that I remember as being ridiculously low and we were back on the highway headed toward Springfield in about an hour and a half.

Does the whole incident sound kind of farfetched to you? Hey, you should read the rest of my writings. That way you could get really *really* offended or saved. :)

This is probably one of the shortest accounts I have written. I cannot begin to enumerate the instances like this that have happened to me over the years and how the LORD has orchestrated rescues in the most incredible ways *every time*.

One of my favorite Psalms is Psalm 91. It just speaks volumes about God and the security, protection and comfort of the believer. I am positive that in the day-to-day living of the believer, there are things averted and thwarted by the love, protection, and power of God and His angels that the person will never even know could have happened. And then there are times of obvious deliverance and rescue that you just *know* beyond any moment of doubt that it was Him. I know for sure that if you love Him with all your heart and put His word first place and final authority in your life, one of these days, if the need arises, He might even give you a sign.

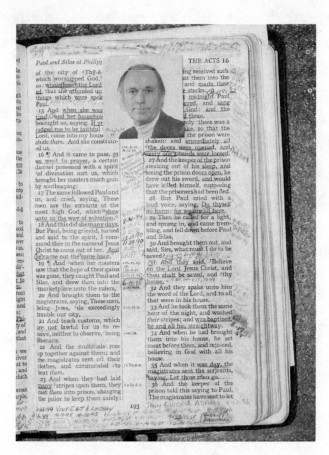

My Dad's picture in Acts 16:31.

You Can Lead a Heart to Water

> But whosoever drinketh of the water that I shall give him shall never thirst; but the water that I shall give him shall be in him a well of water springing up into everlasting life.
>
> John 14:4

If you have been believing, praying, and standing for your family or a loved one's salvation, you need to read this. I know where this is concerned, there is every opportunity to get discouraged because of the way things look, but also consider that it is truly the *will of God* that not one be lost (1 Peter 3:8). The bottom line there is that one way or another, no matter how it looks and no matter how long it takes, with faith and spiritual warfare, *with patience*, you will win. You will.

I got saved back in 1982 and most of my relatives and friends thought I got "too saved," but most of those folks also hadn't been where I had been, nor delivered from what I had been delivered from.

After I found the LORD, I was just ... well ... *thrilled*. I was no longer a stranger from the covenants of promise or having no hope and without God in this world. No. *I finally had it all!*

There are two primary things that happen to the new believer: 1. Ya just have to tell somebody! 2. There's a huge revelation of heaven and eternity. Your heart is sincerely turned to your family, loved ones, and friends. You want them to have what you have. You want the hope of having them in heaven with you.

You need to hear this story about Bill Lichty (lick-tee), my dad.

My dad...long story very short. He was raised by a woman who sure did know the Bible, and scripture could just pour out of her mouth. There was only one problem: she would use the Bible to prove her points, to control, manipulate, and finally get you so confused, you'd just give in! I'm serious, she could plumb wear you out!

So, this is what my dad grew up with, and to say that religion of any kind turned him totally off is a *major* understatement. My mom was a dyed in the wool, very devout Catholic. My dad tolerated it. I was a Catholic 'cause I was raised up into it, but that's a whole 'nother story.

The big thing? Bill Lichty was a genius. For real. He was an engineer extraordinaire and incredibly capable and proficient in all three disciplines: aeronautical, electrical, and structural. There was literally nothing my dad couldn't make fly, electrify, or build. He was amazing.

His first and greatest love was flight. He worked for Douglas Aircraft during the war, which is why he missed the draft back in 1945. Through his career, he worked for Convair, JPL (Jet Propulsion Laboratories), Airlogistics, and finished up retiring from Hughes Aircraft.

If I enumerated the astounding things my dad was part of and accomplished, you'd probably not believe it; from control panels on jets, missile transfer at sea, major contributions in ultraviolet optics, experimental and successful spacecraft to and on the moon. He also had several patented inventions. I could go on and on.

What this all made for is what people like to call "a self-made man," when there really is no such individual. Oh, they think they are, but like Jesus so aptly told Pilate, "You would have no power at all if My Dad hadn't given it to you." That's the "Tell It Like It Is" translation of John 19:11.

You know what else this made for? A man who could not even begin to entertain the idea of anybody more supreme than himself. Genius or whatever, he was always, as far back as I can remember, just *so* difficult to communicate with, 'cause *he* was *right*!

Bill was also a full-blown alcoholic. He and my mom were married for some thirty-five years, but he had countless affairs and women on the side. He didn't claim atheism or agnosticism, but any kind of religious anything was not even an afterthought to him.

I remember enjoying him when I was a child. He taught me to play tennis, which he was remarkably good at. As a matter of fact, there was the tournament when he was scheduled to play Pancho Gonzales but had to drop out 'cause he had pneumonia. (I am serious! The man could do *anything*!)

He taught me how to scuba dive—it was a weekly, sometimes a daily thing—when we lived in La Jolla, California. We did a lot of fishing together. He always had a boat. He taught me how to fly. What a guy. Oh my, and I got my whole sports car thing from my dad. Not just fast cars—no, classic cars—there's a difference. It has stuck with me big all these years.

Sad thing is that he seemed to rapidly lose interest in me when I started having problems with mathematics. He tried teaching me a couple of times, but ended up all frustrated because math was second nature to him but was the farthest from my interest. It was also during that time he became insistent that I call him "Bill" and not Dad or Daddy.

Bill. It was part of the great distance he was fixin' to put between us.

The years went by.

There was a long time after I was out of college and into the work force that Bill and I were totally estranged. He had divorced my mom. She was so sick with arthritis. And I...I was enduring my own alcoholism, failed marriage, stillborn child, nicotine addiction. Please. Dear LORD, I was a mess.

But *light* came! Glory to God! Thank you Father! Oooooh, *thank You*! In my totally fanatical Bible reading travels, I came upon a scripture that to me was the end of all scriptures: Acts 16:31. "Believe on the LORD Jesus Christ and you will be saved and *your house*."

Now, was that sayin' what I thought it was sayin'? *Oh yeah*, and once my heart got a hold of that scripture, (smile) I'm fully persuaded the devil and demons started to tremble!

Even though I hadn't seen my dad in years, I had an old passport picture of him that I dearly loved (yeah, he was really handsome too), and I taped it into my Bible at Acts 16:31. Top of the page. From that day forward, as part of my daily confession (and I do mean "daily"), I started confessing my dad's salvation, and everybody else's too!

> Father, I just want to thank you according to Acts 16:31, that me and my whole household and friends are saved. That among my family and among my friends, we're a family without tragedy. That me, my household, and my friends walk in your divine protection as promised in Psalm 91.

I do not remember how or when it happened (maybe the early 1980s), but I was living in Thousand Oaks, California, at the time, and Bill and his wife, Bea, were living in Huntington Beach, California, about two hours away depending how things were on the San Diego freeway. My dad called me. Wow, out of the clear blue, here I am talkin' to my dad! Just...suddenly here he is on the phone!

He had this idea that we should get together at least once a year to play golf and celebrate our birthdays, which were less than a month apart. Of course I agreed, and it became an instant tradition.

It was somewhat of a head trip seein' him for the first time in about fifteen years, but hey, he was my dad. Occasionally I would see him more than once a year. We rarely spoke on the phone.

In 1987, I moved to Missouri to do prison ministry, and I don't remember what sparked it, don't even remember an initial conversation, but Bill and Bea had decided to come see me in the fall. My dad's coming on an airplane to see me!

This parlayed into a twice-a-year visit with him and Bea. They would come to Missouri in the fall, and I would go out to California in May. We did this for several years, and then in 1998, here comes this phone call from my cousin, Claudia.

Claudia owned a maintenance and janitorial service in Los Angeles that was doing extremely well, and because of my medical technology background and California Clinical Laboratory Scientist licensure, her proposal was that I come out and open a crime scene cleaning division of her service. She was going to make it worth my while. What I heard was liberation from this sweat shop job that I had for ten years, but most of all, I'd be close to my dad and Bea. Bill was in his mid seventies. Getting up there.

Now then, we are going to circumvent all of the stuff having to do with that move. Boy, did I ever have some *massive trash* waitin' for me in California! It was a continual tooth and toenail fight with the devil, but that's another, whole 'nother story.

Every Sunday after church, I would go spend the afternoon with Bill and Bea. We always went out for a nice lunch and then back to their place usually to watch whatever golf tournament that was on, or a movie. Sometimes we'd go down to Bill's boat. It was okay. Yeah, just okay cause my dad's drinking was way out of control. Literally rotting his genius brain away. He would get *so mean*—especially to Bea. I had seen that in him when he and Bea would come to visit me in Missouri, but he was on extra special behavior there. Now he was on his own turf, and oh my, there were so many nice lunches and beautiful Sunday afternoons he ruined. I felt so bad for Bea. Was I still believing for his salvation even though it looked like the most loser thing to do in my whole life? Oh yeah…yeah…for sure. Even more so.

Another tradition, and this one came most naturally: right out of the gate on Sunday when I would walk into their home, I initiated kind of a Praise Report time. I would just start telling 'em what the LORD had done for me that week. Fun stuff. There was always something to share.

At first my dad was real, *real* uncomfortable and maybe even a little bit angered with it. Sigh…perhaps memories of his mom. We would all be standing in the kitchen, and he'd just walk away. But, little by little, he started to kind of hang out. He wasn't always receptive. There were times that he'd look at me in a real disgusted way and say something like, "You really don't believe that junk, do you?"

Eventually, when I would break through those doors, he'd just automatically go sit at the dining room table and very quietly, arms folded, pleasant, patient smile on his face, would assume what I ended up calling his "Praise Report Stance." Pretty cute, really. Those were some of the best moments. 'Course, the rest of the day could have ended up bein' a flamin' disaster, but hey, there was always next Sunday.

Now, there's something I need to interject here 'cause it is very pertinent and actually ended up being a major turning point. Miss Bea is one of twelve siblings. Her eldest sister is a nun, and at the time, Sister Geselda was going to be celebrating her sixtieth year as a nun in the ministry. So...there's the Pope, and then...there's Sister Geselda.

Bea has always been very close to Sister Geselda and occasionally during the Praise Report event, she would mention her. On this particular Sunday, Bea chose to share this card that Sister Geselda had sent to her. It had angels on the front. Female angels. The kind that are all fluffy with large skirts and petty coats, long hair with lots of swirling ribbons, classic huge white wings. You've seen 'em. Countless times.

Okay, so do we really want to be scripturally informative here, or do we want to just ignore it and go on and have a nice day?

Well, it was the female angel thing. Galls me! I have actually *seen* one of my angels, and believe me, he is no sweet, lacy, fluffy, apparition. Barney's *huge* and *intense* and the very *last thing* you would *ever* wanna do is *mess with him*! (Yeah, I'll tell ya about that someday too.)

So, did I blab? Yep. Just a little though. I very quietly said to Miss Bea, "Ya know, if you really look at the Bible, there's no mention of female angels."

My dad just sat there with this sudden cutsie, curious look on his face, waitin' to see what the response was gonna be.

Miss Bea was totally sweet, "Really?" she said with almost childlike disappointment.

"Yeah…yeah, no mention. They're all guys." And that was the end of the conversation.

We did our Sunday afternoon, and on the way home, the LORD started working with me on putting together a little Bible study on angels for next Sunday. As we went through the week, every day He'd show me something really fun and interesting. He really does know this stuff! I was loaded for bear by the time Sunday came.

I'm not gonna go into the study with you, even though it would bless you big. Let it suffice to say, we sat down, Bill had his Praise Report Stance goin' on. Same look. Same patient half smile. Arms folded. I started by telling them that the LORD had shown me some scriptures on angels to share with them.

Miss Bea was very enthusiastic. Bill just stayed in the stance.

Scripture after scripture. Bea would ask intermittent questions. Bill? Stance.

We were just about done, and it came time for me and the Holy Spirit to square off with William Robert Lichty.

"Bill, there's something here you have to see," I started. Just light conversation, but I did have my kind of authoritative voice on. "It's my favorite of all accounts of angelic activity and it's located in Matthew twenty-eight." I turned there and started reading.

> In the end of the Sabbath, as it began to dawn toward the first day of the week, came Mary Magdalene and the other Mary to see the sepulcher. And behold, there was a great earthquake: for the Angel of the LORD descended from heaven, and came and rolled back the stone from the door, and sat upon it.
>
> Matthew 28:1–2

Now I'm lookin' him square in the eyes. "Bill, there was a great earthquake 'for' or *because* the angel of the LORD came. The angel *caused* that earthquake."

He's lookin' at me very skeptically now! I continued, "Angelic beings travel at the speed of light. 186,000 miles a second. That's something you know everything about. And when an angel enters into the earth's atmosphere, he breaks the sound barrier and causes the ground to shake."

If you could have seen the look on his face! I was no longer talking to my stiff-necked dad. No, I was explaining spiritual law and fact to a very accomplished aeronautical engineer! As I talked, you could see it go into his ears, get the stamp of approval from his brain, and from there, it made a direct hit in his heart! *Something about God had finally made sense to him!*

My dad had been blind-sided by God! Gettin' choked up here as I write. He just sat there lookin' at me! There was nothing he could gainsay. What I had explained accurately met all the requirements of physical law. He was stone-still stunned and just stared at me speechless while it was still processing.

The moment abruptly ended when I heard myself cheerfully say (had a big grin on my face), "So there ya have it!" and quickly closed my Bible.

"Oh...well..." Miss Bea chimed in and made some of her sweet, pleasant, chatter. Bill just sat there blankly lookin' at me for the *longest* time. What a day that was. I was *so* encouraged. He had finally heard.

Did he just instantly give his heart to the LORD? No. There was great glory in the moment, but he went back to bein' just Bill.

Strange thing. At the time I'd been in medicine for some thirty-five years and had just about seen it all. My dad really didn't look good to me, and I don't really even remember when that revelation started to come. He looked okay when I first got to California in 1998. I figured that he had at least a good fifteen years left on him. And see, I never really was close to him. It's not like I could just say something like, "Bill, are you feelin' all right? You don't look good. Let's get ya in to see a doctor." No...no. By the time November of 2000 was upon us, he had a noticeable pallor. Seems he had lost a little weight too, and then he took sick with some sort of really nasty flu-like syndrome. Multiple visits to the doctors. He had a couple of biopsies. His lungs were filling with fluid. As time wore on, after treatment with heavy artillery antibiotics, steroids, and a diuretic, he actually seemed to be getting better. I remember being concerned, praying and believing for his healing, but not spiritually distressed in any way about it. Then came Christmas.

Christmas Day 2000. I went over to Bill and Bea's to enjoy the day. When I walked in, I saw the look on Bill's face. He asked me and Bea to have a seat at the dining room table. This was not a Praise Report event.

The man never wasted words, and that day was no exception. He had been to the doctor and was told he had twelve weeks to live.

Melanoma. Satan's perfected cellular chaos. His chest x-ray looked like his lungs were filled with buckshot, which was, in fact, metastasized cancer. They had no idea where the primary lesion was, and weren't gonna go lookin' for it. The doctor told him to just go home and he'd be in touch. That was all he had to say, and wow, I was so taken aback!

You know, it was like at that moment, the scales had suddenly fallen away from my eyes and I could actually see him. He had been slowly wasting away before our eyes. I did not go into medical mode with questions and suggestions and all that ensues from that. My dad was dying.

Have you ever felt like you've suddenly walked into the wrong room? I was a silent, subdued wreck. Bea was totally numb. And you know we did the most bizarre thing: Bill put Christmas dinner on the table and we ate. We sat there like three little drones. I don't even remember opening our gifts. All I remember is the drive home that night.

I'm fixin' to say something to you right now that's probably going to sound kind of mercenary. No, pragmatic may be a better choice of words. We're gonna take a moment out here for some teaching so you'll understand the motivation and what prompted the decisions that needed to be made. I suddenly found my heart in a very difficult and hurtful situation.

There are *times*...takin' my time here to word this correctly...There *will be* times that you're going to have to be very direct and hurtfully honest with yourself about what you truly believe and what you are capable of standing on. You also may have to take into very grave consideration what other people who are involved in the situation are believing or "say" that they believe. I cannot stress what a biggie that is. These are the finite, exact points of a successful walk of faith.

A real glaring fact is that Jesus said so many times, "According to *your* faith be it done unto you," or "*Your* faith has saved you." Now granted, there is the incredible, loving, *most gracious* power of God in doing miracles on our behalf, but we were not made to live from one miracle to another. The faith walk got it done for Jesus. He spent three years showing us how to do it, and part of His legacy of salvation is that the faith walk will get whatever we need to be done for us too.

Faith is also a living thing. You have to feed your faith on a daily basis just the way you feed your physical body. According to Jesus, there are levels of faith: great, little, and no faith. It's a fluctuating spiritual force, and what you use, you have to replace. I've seen people (and have done it *just once* myself) who have experienced great faith victories and then become complacent. You could say, "They have faith in their faith." The reality? *Yesterday's faith does not make for tomorrow's victories.*

There, that's all the preachin' I'm gonna do, and I won't even take up an offering. :)

Driving home that night, there was *all-out war* in my heart! My was mind goin' a million miles a minute. Drivin' along just non-stop blabbin' out loud to myself. All choked up. Tryin' not to cry. Bless the LORD, the devil *was not* gonna see me cry over this!

The burning question to myself from me was this, "Penny, are you gonna believe God to heal Bill? We are lookin' at a major faith expenditure here. You capable of doin' this without being moved by the circumstances *at all*? He's eighty years old. You suppose this is what *he* wants? They've given him twelve weeks! You capable of listenin' to all the doom and gloom from the doctors? They'll trample you! You suppose Bill and Bea are really gonna be comforted and edified by a positive confession of faith? At this point, it will appear to be totally insane to them. And the pain! Watchin' him suffer will totally *break* you!"

On and on. See, I'm countin' the cost here. Faith is something you have to use very much on purpose.

I remember exactly where I was along Beach Boulevard that night when effectual, fervent prayer began to easily flow from my heart across my lips. Told the LORD I could sure believe Him for a miracle, but really what I sorely wanted more than anything was to have a manifestation of Acts 16:31 that I had been believing and confessing for almost twenty years. I wanted to *see* my dad's salvation and have the assurance that he would be in heaven.

There was also one special request: no pain. I have seen cancer patients suffer so hard and long. It was so heavy on my heart as I asked God please to remove all physical suffering so Bill could be comfortable and Bea and I wouldn't be in a continual atmosphere of torment—that he could just peacefully "drift" on out of here. With the "amen" came such a feeling of relief. I was good with it.

When I finally crawled into bed that night, this revelation came. God hadn't moved me out there to extricate me from the ongoing problems I had or so I could be some crime-scene-cleaning honcho. No, it was solely to be able to take care of my dad while he was dying. With that, my heart became strongly established in what was needful for me to do, and I set a course that night to begin our walk through that Psalm 23 valley.

The following day (and I really don't mean to be graphic or offensive here, but if you don't know what was happening, then you'll not really appreciate the miracles that started to follow) Bill had started bleeding very badly from his kidneys. His urine was solid blood with clots. Bea took him to the local emergency room. They contacted his doctor, started him on an antibiotic, and actually give him a unit of blood. Then they told him, very matter of fact, that would be all the blood they'd be giving him for the duration. He was given these positively huge trans-dermal morphine patches and then they simply sent him home. They literally just wrote him off! I was furious! In all my years of medicine, I've never seen that done to a patient. Even if he only had a few days to live, you just don't do that! Wow, and now I'm having the perfect opportunity to walk in forgiveness of these people!

The next day, his urine miraculously started to clear up, and by the following day, he was normal. The antibiotic? (smile) I don't think so.

That evening we had a light dinner together, and I told them that I would be more than happy to come over in the afternoon after I got off work to help with his care—spend the night if need be. That he wasn't goin' to any nursing home. We'd all be just fine right here. The suggestion was well and gratefully received.

We began to pace ourselves through the days. A great and very unexpected gift is my dad just suddenly stopped drinking. For real. I finally had my dad. Praise God. It made everything so much easier. He was kind and grateful and very compliant with what needed to be done. Amazing. Thank you, LORD.

And those humungous pain patches? There they sat in plain sight on his desk. That's where they stayed too.

There was one afternoon that Bill and I were up in his den, and he was trying to teach me to use his drafting arm to measure off a mat for a picture frame. I wasn't doing as well as he'd like, which was always the case, and then suddenly he did this deep sigh and said so regretfully, "I have never been a very good teacher."

"Bill, you're a great teacher, just not a very patient one." I continued with a smile, "Most people, myself included, aren't as smart as you are and things come a bit slower to us. But you're fine."

Had I seen a moment of humility in my dad? Yes, and perhaps it was a kind of subtle apology too. It was a moment of closeness that I don't remember having ever had with him. And then I heard myself say, "Have you thought about God and Jesus and heaven at all?"

His answer: "Let's not talk about that now." Not in a mean way. He just kindly didn't want to talk about it right then.

I kind of leaned into him and smiled, "That's okay. But you need to know that it sure wouldn't be heaven without ya."

There were afternoons I'd go over and Bill would have his boat cronies or his work friends over visiting. Wow, heavy brass from work, some he hadn't seen in years comin' to pay their respects. He would have one beer to celebrate their presence and talk with them. I never saw him drunk again. What a *gift*. Those were actually very good days for him.

Later in the evening we'd get him into bed. We would bathe him. Eventually he did reach the point where he needed a diaper. It was taken in stride by all of us.

What was difficult is you could actually almost watch those melanoma tumors grow on him. It was like watching zucchini grow in the garden. Those things would come up so fast on him. The memory of it still astounds me. But the LORD was so faithful: Bill had no pain. None. Praise God.

And Bea, bless her. Just always a stalwart. Always ready to do whatever was needful. She and I would have a nice kind of quiet time before I left for the night. She'd make a snack. We'd visit and maybe watch a little television. It was such a blessing to have each other.

The days turned into weeks, and Bill became bedridden. The hospice ladies started to come. Of course his care was more intense, but he was still able to think and express himself. There was finally the afternoon...

It was January 29, 2001. I had just come to their house, and the very moment I walked through the door, I could feel this...the best way to describe it is a spirit of unrest. There was a ton of spiritual activity, and I didn't know it right then but we were fixin' to show the devil that *Jesus is, in fact,* LORD!

I went upstairs, and Bill was visibly agitated. First time I'd seen him that way since he'd been sick. I started his bath, and for a moment there, I think he actually didn't know who I was. I continued bathing and talking to soothe and comfort. I was over at the sink rinsing out his wash cloth. The LORD spoke to me, "He's quiet now." I turned and looked at Bill and answered the LORD out loud, "Yeah, he is."

At that moment I knew it was time. I walked over to him and kneeled next to the bed and softly asked, "Bill, would you like to make Jesus Christ the LORD of your life now?"

He nodded yes to me.

And then, a twenty-year prayer-battle finally came to pass. I prayed with my dad, and he did speak those celebrated words. With the "amen" I saw this peace flow into him. Oh my, and the peace that came flooding over me! Peace and *untold* relief!

Hey, and you may be sittin' there reading this and thinkin' that my dad just said the prayer cause he knew it meant so much to me or as some sort of fire insurance. Why would you even want to minimize or make slight of such a precious miracle? You will have missed the incredible demonstration of the mercy and love of God. Besides, I was there with him. I saw the miraculous changes in his countenance after we prayed. His eyes were no longer filled with death even though he was dying.

I am convinced that it was my ongoing confession that withstood the test of time and circumstance; and all the doubt, unbelief, and traumatic situations the devil tried to pummel me with to get me to quit. The reward was exactly what I confessed and believed for all those years and a *major validation* of the *Love* and *faithfulness* of *God:* my dad's salvation! Glory to the name of the LORD!

The following days were absolutely precious. Bill was upstairs in his bed just driftin.' No pain. In the evenings, I'd perch beside him in the bed and read the Bible to him.

Then came that Tuesday afternoon. The hospice nurse was upstairs with him, and Bea and I were downstairs eating lunch. We both suddenly saw the nurse standing on the landing, "You'd better come."

I wanted to bound up those stairs, but Bea and I walked them together.

At first look, I thought for sure Bill had gone, but no, the nurse said his heart was still beating and it wouldn't be long.

I crawled up in the bed with him, held him, told him that I loved him, and started praying in the spirit as he was breathing his last breaths. A goodbye honor and comfort I will never forget.

Strange. I have never cried over the passing of my mom or my dad, but I'm sittin' here now doing exactly that. They are not tears of grief or loss. No, they are tears in memory and celebration of my dad's home-going and the incredible goodness and faithfulness of such a loving, patient, *good* God. I truly believe that once my heart got a hold of Acts 16:31 and I started confessing it, that things started to move in the spirit world. The LORD *honors His word* and had gradually started walking me toward March 13, 2001, the day of my dad's eternal life.

And this, (sigh) brings us back to the beginning: believing for your loved one's salvation. Look at Acts 16:31 on purpose for yourself. Confess it daily and even more frequently if that particular individual is giving you opportunity to walk in anger and unforgiveness toward them. You may have to leave the room to do it, but *do it*! The devil is not going to give up without a fight. But *you* be stalwart! *You* be faithful! *You* be unwavering! You fight him just the way Jesus did on the mount of temptation: with *the word of God*! Your reward is *victory*, a major manifestation of the Love of God, and a loved one's passport to Heaven.

If you have never made Jesus Christ the LORD of your life and you're experiencing a real heart tug right now, the prayer is short and simple. It's really quite amazing that so few words when spoken from the heart can make the difference in one's final destination and eternal life. I encourage you, do not to let this precious moment pass you by.

Just pray these words out loud.

Dearest Heavenly Father, in the name of Jesus I come before you and confess that I have been miss-

ing the mark so badly. I ask you to forgive my sins. I confess that Jesus lived on this earth, died for my sins, and rose from the dead that I might have eternal life with you in Heaven. Come into my heart now, lord Jesus. I make you lord over all that I am, think, say, and do. You are lord of my life. In Jesus's name, amen.

If you just prayed and received Jesus, *congratulations*! You have caused a great celebration in heaven and your name is now written in the Lamb's Book of Life. Welcome to the family of God!

From here, please get yourself a Bible that is easy for you to understand. Your local Christian bookstore can be of great help there. Start reading at the New Testament so you can get to know Jesus. Also of great importance is that you get into a good Bible-based church and start enjoying your brand new life with your new family! What a thrill! I'll be prayin' for you!

A lovely addendum to this story: It wasn't until a few weeks ago that it suddenly came to me that I had written in one of the closing paragraphs "and a loved one's passport to heaven." The picture that was taped into my Bible for all of those years was, in fact, a genuine passport picture. The Bible in Isaiah 46:10 says that God "declares the end from the beginning." I can't even begin to fathom that one morning in 1982, at the very moment I was taping the passport picture into Acts 16, God was declaring the answer. Through all of those years, the victory was already there.